WILLOW PUBLICATIONS (DUBLIN)

With Love from Pat

PAT INGOLDSBY

POEMS
SO FRESH
AND SO NEW
...YAHOO!

D1585988

First published in 1995
by Willow Publications (Dublin),
3 Vernon Court,
Seafield Road West,
Clontarf, Dublin 3,
EIRE.

Cover Artwork/Invaluable Help: Steve Averill
Front Cover: Photo by Kate Sawyer
Back Cover: Photo by Chris Lacey
Best Boy: Hoot
Muddy Pawmarks: Willow
Inspiration: God
Hard Words: My Dictionary

ISBN: 0 9523052 16
Printed in Ireland by Colour Books Ltd.

Maureen Forde...thank you for reintroducing me to courage, humour, love and roguery... this book is for you.

With my love,

PAT

Clontarf January 1995.

Contents

SURPRISED BY SPRING

Would you look!
Just look at the trees!
I have never seen so much blossom.
It is billowing the branches.
It is billowing and bridesmaiding
and filling up and filling out the trees
with so much cream and so much froth
that one good gust of of wind
would blitz the skies with such a blizzard
of white and yellow and orange
that it would make you dizzy
just to look at it.

Would you look!
Just look at the trees!
All the colours are so fresh and bright and new
that if you tipped them you would wet your finger
with the feel of fresh wet Nature paint.
Splashes of brightest yellow
blinding white
and the deepest richest most intoxicating orange
that I have ever seen.
Even the blackbird's beak is not as bright
as the orange on the branches.
All the tiny birds hiding in the hedges
are swelling up with the thrill
of their very first Spring song.

I am amazed because the sights
and the sounds are taking me by surprise
the way that they always do.
I have never yet experienced
a Spring or a Summer which does not seem
like the very first one that I ever knew.

Later in the evening when it is quiet
I am looking towards the West
and the fading sky is pink and blue
and I do not mind the night.
Today for the 52nd time
I have seen my very first Spring
and smiled with pleasure
because it always seems so childlike
and it always seems so right.

Thank you for the Tumble

Tinkle tinkle
tumble tumble
fingers rushing
to the end of
the keyboard
and cascading
into the upward
coming surge
of the orchestra
and Edvard Grieg
you are bloody
BRILLIANT!

BLUE FLOWERS BY THE SKITTERYDILLION

I couldn't think of a number
to describe the millions
and billions and trillions
of tiny blue flowers which
I saw in the field
so I am going to call it
a skitterydillion.
For the benefit of mathematicians
who like to have everything exact
and precise and quantified
I hereby decree that when
it comes to tiny blue flowers
there are 5.675 zillion of them
in a skitterydillion.
It you don't believe me
you can always count them.

THIS IS MY SONG

A small old man with a crooked eye
and excitement on his face
and no money in his pocket
said to me – "I wrote a song once.
I wrote it 20 years ago and I still
remember it. I didn't write it down
or anything like that because it
hasn't got any words."

Then he sang it for me.
"Lah lah lah lah lah lah
  lah lah lah lah lah lah
  lah lah lah lah lah lah."

He said that he knows it so well
he can start it in the middle
and sing it to the end.
He said that he knows it so well
he can sing it backwards.
He said that it's his song
and he will never forget it.

He said wouldn't it be great
if someone played it on a piano.
Or a guitar.
Or anything at all.

He said that he might write another
one someday.
And then he went away
with his head and his heart
full of his song.

Oooh it was Red!

Suddenly the night was flooded
with deep rich red.
The traffic lights splashed
the wet road with the deepest
richest red that I have ever seen
and the raindrops on the window
of the bus were drops of blood
and the red lights on the cars
reached down into the wetness
of the road with wild kisses
of crimson and I was dizzy
with the delight of so much
unexpected red richness.
I walked up Vernon Avenue
and the rain was slow mist
and the street lights caressed
the dark wetness of the road
with so much bright yellow
and light lemon that I was
crazy with the thrill
of looking at it.
Oooooh it was red!
Oooooh it was yellow!
Oooooh it was night time
and I was dizzy with delight.

You would probably need special paint

Wouldn't it be lovely
to paint a hole in your floor
which looks so real
that people drop pebbles into it
and ten seconds later
they hear a splash.

SHINY BLACK DIVER

One minute the cormorant was swimming
in the Liffey.
Then he dived under the water
and he was gone.
I stood on Butt Bridge and watched
and waited and wondered
where he would pop up again.
I waited for ages.
Then I started to worry.
My God – maybe he's in trouble.
Maybe he crashed into a very big fish
on the way down
and knocked himself out.
Maybe he was fed up being a cormorant
all by himself in the Liffey
and he decided to end it all.
Maybe I should strip to the waist
and dive in and rescue him.

"Please come up again cormorant.
  Please come up."

I think he must have heard me.
He suddenly popped up again
down near O'Connell Bridge.

"Thanks be to God."

I really didn't want to jump in.
Well not today anyway.

Some poets write poems
which I can't make
head or tail of
and other people
come along and write
reviews of the poems
which are equally
bewildering.
Nobody has got a clue
what the poems mean
and nobody has got a clue
what the reviews mean
so everybody says that
they are brilliant
and deep and meaningful
even though nobody
has got the faintest idea
what the meaning is
and that is The Arts.
As far as I am concerned
you can keep it.
This poem is not The Arts
and it doesn't want to be.
This next section is though.

"The ineffable seeking of
  Life's self-perpetuating
  search for itself."

I don't know what that means
even though I have just
written it which proves
that I can write stuff
which is The Arts
if I put my mind to it.
What a truly terrifying
thought.

WINTER SUNSET AT CLONTARF

A blinding ball
of cold iced lemon
sent a strip
of yellow light
across the top
of the wet sand
and you would shiver
just to look at it.

Edging towards the End

There is nobody in the house now.
The television has gone back to
the shop.
The fridge has been emptied and
the plug has been pulled out.
Nobody walks up and down the stairs
anymore.
My mother has gone into a home.
Her mind splutters and fits and
starts.
Sometimes she understands and
sometimes she doesn't.
Sometimes she keeps asking
"What time is it?"
Once she asked – "Where have all
the children gone?"
Some of the lights behind her eyes
are switched off now and she only
sees fragments of things.
My brother bought her a watch with
a very large face on it
but she still keeps asking
"What time is it?"
Whatever the time is now
it is a very long time ago.

My father is sixteen years gone.
My mother is living in a home.
Nobody is walking up and down
the stairs anymore.

It is nearly finished.

WELL ENOUGH ALONE

I always thought that a daisy
is a very little flower.
Then I looked over a wall
into somebody's garden
and I saw these
tiny little blue flowers
which are much smaller
than a daisy is.
The daisies probably love them.
Perhaps there are even tinier
flowers than the blue ones.
If so, they must be extremely
teenchy indeed.
A bee certainly couldn't land on one.
A bee couldn't even land on the blue ones.
In fact, if I was a bee I wouldn't even
chance landing on a daisy.
But Mother Nature knows exactly
what she is doing.
Left to her own devices
she has no trouble whatsoever
working these things out.
Neither do the bees
or the blue flowers
or the daisies.

Well enough alone.

SLOPEY COWS
(not to be confused with sloppy which is a very different
thing altogether)

Slopey cows lie down
on slopey hills
a lot of the time.
In fact they lie
on the slopes
for so long
that when
their milk comes out
it is slopey too.
You can always tell
when milk is slopey
just by looking at it.
The level at the top
is slanted.
I'm not sure what
would happen
to rashers
if pigs started
to lie down on
slopes as well.
I suppose you could
always ask somebody.

Safe Sex with Irish Music

She danced a hornpipe
on my thumb
all night
and she was sitting
down.

I'm asking Myself

Where is the point in having a rocking chair
if you don't sit in it and rock?
Where is the point in having taps
in your house if you don't hold your hands
under them and feel the water flowing
in between your fingers?
Where is the point in putting pictures
on your wall if you don't stop and look
and see what is in them?
Where is the point in having wind
if you don't do lovely loud farts?
Where is the point in having arms
if you don't put them around somebody?
If you don't have anybody
put them around yourself.
Always and forever
no matter who or how
or where you are
you deserve a hug.

Oh yes you do!

STICK ME UP A CHIMNEY OR SOMEWHERE

When I die
please don't bury me
in a graveyard
full of people
because that's not
how my life was.

He Comes and Goes

Sometimes a big black spider wanders out
from behind my bookshelves.
He comes out at night for a ramble
around my Superser.
Sometimes he stops in the middle
of the carpet and he thinks
about things for a while.
Then he wanders in behind my bookshelves
again.
I'd love to know what it's like in there.
I wonder has he got little chairs and a table.
I wonder has he got a patchwork quilt.
I don't really know and I don't think
it would be right to look.
Sometimes a big black spider wanders out
from behind my fridge in the kitchen.
He is the image of the one who lives
in behind the bookshelves.
He is exactly the same size and he walks
the same way and everything.
Perhaps they are twins.
Perhaps it's not two spiders at all.
Perhaps it's the same one and he lives
in two different places.
I don't really know.
They all look the same to me.
Perhaps we all look the same to them
as well.
I don't really know that either.

NOWHERE YOU COULDN'T GO

Do you remember
when you sat alone
in a hot lazy field
and thought about a place
millions of miles away
and you felt yourself
filling up with the wonder
and the mystery of the thought?
The sky curved away
into a perfect dome
and you thought about a place
far beyond it
and something mysterious
stirred inside you.
You could hear the sounds
of the village
and you knew them all
but there was something else
so huge and immense
that you got the strangest
feeling.
It was scary
and it was exciting.
Do you remember?
It was summer.
It was childhood.
It was wonder.
It was you.

GOD KNOWS

Willow is the gingerest
            gentlest
                cat
That I have ever known.
He lies on his back
and offers me his tummy.
He knows that I will
never hurt him.
He tells me things
with his meows.
I know from the sound
of them that it is good.
He shares my house
and rubs his head
against my chin
when I am sad.

I think that God
was at His very finest
when he created gentle
            ginger
             cats.
He knows that it was good
and so do I.

AND WE WOULD COLOUR THE PICTURES

When we were very little
and lived so close to the sea
that it came in under the front door
Aunty Alice gave me a colouring book.
There were pictures of boys and girls
playing hopscotch
and skipping
and chasing.
Beside each child
was a very tall Guardian Angel
who they couldn't see.
The angel had huge white wings
feathered like a seagull's.

My mother was a young slender woman
with long auburn hair
who would turn every head in the village
and she strode out with her wicker
shopping basket.
And we coloured in the pictures.

My mother is a long way from the sea now.
Her sight and her speech are almost gone.
My sister tucks her into bed at night
and kisses her forehead.
There is nothing else that she
or anybody else can do.

Maybe there is a golden light
around her bed
which none of us can see.
Maybe there are huge white wings
feathered like a seagull's.
Maybe there is sea and there is sand
to take her fright away.
We would love to colour in
all these pictures for her
if we only knew how.
We look at her instead
and wonder what it is
that she is seeing.

Your Exercise for Today
(N.B. Do a gentle warm-up first)

Go and gallop on a wild horse
and hold onto its mane
and thunder down
the longest beach
in and out of the waves
in and out of the water.

Run into a forest
where you have never been
and crack the twigs
with your eager
frightened feet.
Catch a high branch
and swing on it.
Race down one side
of a mossy ditch
and up the other.
Whistle back at the birds
and chase a dizzy rabbit
round in circles.

Shout into a deep dark cave
and laugh at the echoes.

Look up at a clear bright moon
and wander around the heavens
with your eyes.

Race down a steep hill
until the headlong slope
makes you run
faster that you are able.

Stand so still
for so long
that all the voices
go away
and there is nothing left
to come between you
and the feel of who
you truly are.

Now start again!

MORE CHEAPER THAN A PHONE CALL

If you dip your finger into the sea
at Dollymount Strand
as far as I am concerned
you are making indirect contact
with India and Australia
and places like that.

Supposing that the woman you love
is in North Africa
and you are in Ireland.
You could both agree on an exact time
when you dip your hand into the Irish Sea
and she dips hers into the Mediterranean
and you both waggle them to and fro
and send ripples towards one another.

It is truly romantic and deeply symbolic
and you will never become pregnant
no matter how much waggling you do.

It will give you both
an acute sense of togetherness
unless a shark comes along
and bites off your fingers
while you are doing it.

Love hurts.

The scream of the gull
will fill me up
and I will see
what the white gull sees
when it looks down unblinking
from a dizzy height
and the tips of its wings
will touch me
high on empty air
and I will whizz with white
and skim the crashing rocks
instead of walking slow
beside them.

And I will not drown.

The scream of the gull
will fill me up
and I will feel
what the white gull feels
when it lets the wind take it
and you don't know where
you are rising next
or falling
but the wind does
and you are gliding
on the highest high
or diving dizzy down.

And I will not drown.

The scream of the gull
will fill me up
and I will hear
what the white gull hears
when the sky is wild
and seaspray spits
and I will speed
split-seconds
from the deepest green
and fill the spaces
in between
with a wild screech
of freedom.

And I will not drown.

Everytime I see a gull
I will look up
and let my spirits fly.
Everytime I see a gull
I will look up
and glory
in the giddy gladness
of fingertipping towards
the highest high.

HOW IT HAILED

Hailstones making split-second bubbles
where they hit the wet grey
some of them hitting
and spitting straight up again
with a wicked ricochet.
Some of them stinging
and pin-pricking your face
millions of them diving down
and dancing themselves to death
in a dizzy dancing race.

STARTING TO FEEL THAT I BELONG

And I will pick up
the pink blossom
from the grass
where it has fallen
and fling it up
into the wind.

And I will smash
my hand down on
top of the water
and feel the sting
and watch the silver
sparkles explode
into the sky.

And I will stand
among the trees
at dark and wait
till the birdsong
stops
and I will listen
to the deeper
silence.

And I will wrap
my arms around a tree
and try to feel
the suck and flow

of juices
from the earth
and I will touch
rough bark
with the softness
of my cheek.

And I will wait
until the wind
is strong enough
to make full mountains
under ships
far out at sea
and I will lean
into its fury
and trust it
to take my weight.

And I will feel at one
with all the creatures
who walk and swim
and crawl and fly
and I will rejoice
that I belong
as much as they
and they as much as I.

It is not Funny

If I don't wear a contraceptive
you will get what's coming
and it might be more than that.

An awful lot more.

CHATTER CHATTER TWITCH TWITCH

Whenever one of my cats
looks at a bird
his teeth begin to chatter
and his whiskers twitch.

He can't help himself.

It is involuntary.

I wish that exactly
the same thing happened
with humans.

If you look at somebody
and you fancy them
straight away
your teeth begin to chatter
and your whiskers twitch.
You can't help yourself.
It just happens.

Chatter chatter
twitch twitch
meow meow
me too
yahooooo!

THE BLUES

He fitted up all his gear.
And set up the amps and speakers.
He tuned his guitar
and slipped his harmonica
into his holder
and then he waited.
In the empty pub
for sixty long minutes
he waited
but nobody came.

He picked up his guitar
and he played the blues.
He played the most
deep down melancholy blues
that ever brought condensation
creeping out of the walls.
He played and he sang
all the things
which he needed to sing
and there was nobody there
to hear them.

Then he performed an encore
because the empty pub
deserved it.

WELCOME HOME

Today
for the very first time
in 52 years
I wish to propose
a sincere vote of thanks
to my skin and my blood
and my fingernails
and my heart and my lungs
and every other part of me
both big, medium, small and tiny.

You must have thought that
I'd never get round to it.

52 years of breathing and pumping
and pulsing and regenerating
and there was me taking
all the credit.

I don't know how to grow a toenail.
You do.

I haven't got a clue how to digest
a Brussel Sprout.
You do.

I haven't got the remotest idea
how to orchestrate a hiccup.
You do.

You know things
which are a million years
older than me
yet I have never even
sent you a birthday card.

Today for the very first time
I am calling you friend.

Today for the very first time
I am falling in love with you.

Today for the very first time
I am alive to the millions
of miracles which are me.

I love it
when people tell me things
off the record.

I asked a waiter
about the large bladed fan
which was whizzing around
overhead.

"If that thing comes off
  do you have any idea of
  its appropriate flight path?"

"Don't quote me on this Pat
  but it would probably fly
  straight out through the
  fucking window."

I will only quote him the once.
Here.
Now.
Let that be an end to it.

"Securicor Cares."
That is what it said
on the side of the security van.

"Excuse me" I asked the men
with the blue helmets.
"On the side of Brink's Allied vans
  it says – 'We More Than Care.'
  Does this mean that they care
  more than you do?"

"Basically speaking Pat,
  we couldn't give a bollix."

What a magnificent logo to emblazon
on the side of your vans.

"WE COULDN'T GIVE A BOLLIX"

I would happily entrust my life savings
to a company with that level of honesty.

Bollix is right.

NOT GUILTY

This bottle of whiskey
is accused
of wrecking my marriage
   alienating me from my family
   losing me all my money
   and completely wrecking my life.

That is one hell of a guilt trip
to lay on a glass bottle.

One of the Poor Girls must be Sick

A young nun was walking up Vernon Avenue
towards me.
She paused.
She cleared her throat.
She released an unmerciful spit
which whacked against the pavement.
I have never seen anything like it
in my life.
I know it's not mentioned
in the Ten Commandments
but I didn't think that nuns
are supposed to spit like that.
Not unless you are a member
of a brand new break-away order
called "The Little Sisters
of the Supersonic Spit."
You'd be expected to do it then.

I told the woman in the cleaners
what I had seen.
"She'd probably swallowed a fly"
she said.
You'd have to.

God alone knows what you would get for a huge Big Brent Goose or an Ostrich

I met a man downtown today
who told me that he is swopping
his budgie for a mountain bike.

I am not making this up.
He took off his dark glasses
and looked into my eyes
and said – "I am swopping
my budgie for a mountain bike."

That is one hell of a rate
of exchange.

That is infinitely more exciting
than boring dollar and sterling
charts.

Let us draw up a new currency
based on the simple equation
"One budgie equals one mountain bike."
Let us take it from there.
Let us put birdsong and wheelies
into banking.

Coins can't sing.

It's All the One

There are two signs
at O'Connell Bridge
both pointing
in exactly
the same direction
down Aston Quay.

One says – "The West."
One says – "The South."

I love that.

SOMETIMES UNDER CERTAIN CONTROLLED CONDITIONS A RELEASE OF FLATULENCE IN YOUR BACK YARD CAN LEAD TO SPONTANEOUS PRAYER

I sometimes like to sit outside
on top of my coal bunker
at four o'clock in the morning
and let fly with a fierce
ripsnorter of a fart
which resounds with a deep full
metallic boom.
Some of my neighbours
who are lying awake in their beds
sit up suddenly and exclaim –
"Good heavens – that must be some
  fog at sea. God bless all mariners
  and bring them safely back to shore."

Blessed are they who fart on top
of their coal bunkers
for they shall be called foghorns.

TOO LATE

Too late
Henry Rosthimble realised
he was sharing his tent
with a giant shortsighted
strawberry.

Too late
Henry Rosthimble realised
that the strawberry
had mistaken him
for a very attractive
strawberry
of the opposite sex.

Too late
Henry Rosthimble realised
that immediately after mating
the giant shortsighted
strawberry
eats its partner.

Next morning
his loyal manservants
ate the shortsighted
strawberry
for breakfast.

Then they organised
a search-party
and went into the jungle
to try and find
Henry.

BLIND COWS CAN'T HEAR

In the land
behind the wardrobe
in your bedroom
all the cows moo
at one another
with speech balloons
so that you won't know
they are there.

MISTER HOLLOW HAYSTACKS

I met an old man in Grafton Street
who used to build hollow haystacks.
He also built walls with holes in them
but the hollow haystacks were the best.

"There'd be two soldiers hiding inside
each one" he said.

Two soldiers with guns inside
a pretend haystack
waiting for the Germans.
There would be lots of other haystacks
in the field but they were real ones.
The invading German army would say
"Mein Goth – what a beautiful field
full of lovely real haystacks."
They would unpack their
brightly coloured gingham table-cloths
and sit down to enjoy a picnic.

Suddenly a hidden voice would say
"Hands up! Throw down those sandwiches!"
And the Third Reich would surrender
to a hollow haystack.

"But they never came" he said.
"The soldiers waited for years
inside me hollow haystacks
and they waited for years
behind me walls with holes in them
but the Germans never came."

He got work in Dublin
french-polishing the dance floor
in The Metropole
until they knocked it down.
Now he walks around the city all day
until they come to knock him down too.
It's bad enough being old
but Sundays are the worst.
Nobody wants a hollow haystack.

BLOOD ON BLUE

I cut myself in three places
while I was shaving yesterday
and I walked around the house
with little pieces
of blue tissue paper
attached to my face.

One by one
they came free
and fluttered
to the floor
and lay there
like single-petalled
blue flowers
with a bright red spot
in the middle.

No offence little chestnut
but would you ever fuck off
back to wherever it is
you came from.
It's only June.
You're not due until the Autumn.
My life is going fast enough as it is
without bloody chestnuts in June.
I realise that there is only the one
of you
but if this sort of thing catches on
there will be bloody conkers
bursting out all over the place
and then were will I be?
How would you like it
if I started throwing sticks up at you
right now?
That's what people do in the Autumn.
You're throwing sticks at me
just by being there.
Fair is fair.
Take your time.
There's no rush.
Honestly.
Autumn will be here.
I mightn't.
But Autumn will.

So relax.

Stay as tiny as you are.

Enjoy the summer.

Oh ... and about the sticks.

Don't worry.

I always missed anyway.

I HOPE SO

I think that cars
have got treads
in their tyres
so they won't crush
beetles and earwigs
and ants.

At least I hope
that's the reason.

Your Babies are Crying

Today
I saw such a celebration
of white flowers
that I stopped and looked
for little orange ladybirds
with black spots on their wings.
I looked for a long time
but I couldn't find one.

When
my brother David was very small
he wandered away and got lost.

When
we found him he was hidden
among tall white flowers
which were even higher
than the top of his fair head.

His hands were filled with ladybirds.
They were crawling between his fingers.
They were resting on his palms.
They were walking up his arm.
His eyes were full of the wonder
of them.

David lives in Canada now.
He is gone away
and no matter how hard I look
I cannot find any ladybirds.

He couldn't answer That

Today I lifted the lid
of my wicker laundry basket
and saw a man sitting inside it.

"How did you get in there?"

"I hid in the pocket of your jeans."

"But you'd never fit."

"Oh."

THE TIME HAS COME

It is high time we started to feed
our negative thoughts the same sort
of negative stuff that they give us.

"Dear negative thought,
  supposing that you collide
  with another negative thought
  and become a POSITIVE!!
  What will you do then?"

That's the stuff to give them.

OTHER HAND ON HIS STICK

It is eleven o'clock in the morning
in North Earl Street.
A clock around the corner
is pealing "Somewhere my Love."
James Joyce is standing stiffly
outside the Cafe Kylemore
with his left hand in his pocket.
Whatever he is doing with it
is his own business entirely.
He is staring fixedly
across O'Connell Street
at the G.P.O.
His other hand is on his stick.
That's the right place to have it.

A POEM ABOUT TRAINEE HARD MEN FROM POSH UPPER MIDDLE CLASS FAMILIES WHO PUT ON PHONY DUBLIN WORKING CLASS ACCENTS AND PRAY TO GOD THAT THEY WON'T MEET THEIR SISTER WHILE THEY ARE OUT WITH THEIR MATES BECAUSE IF SHE SPEAKS TO HIM IN THE WAY THAT THE FAMILY USUALLY SPEAKS HIS COVER WILL BE BLOWN

(This title is probably longer than the poem but that doesn't really matter)

Trainee hard man
13 years of age
they spit a lot
lunge their heads a lot
say 'Fuck' and 'Shit' a lot
call their house a 'gaff'
or better still
'a fucking gaff'
do daring things
like starting fires
in litter bins
wear jackets with
'Los Angeles Raiders'
on the back
and go home
at six o'clock
for their tea.

THIS IS ALL THAT I KNOW ABOUT HER

She came over the brow
of the hill in Dingle
and the summer grass
was touching her feet.

I never knew her name.

The sun behind her
was shining through
her cotton-thin dress
and showing the
shadow-shape of her body.

The wind off the sea
flirted with her red hair
and she stood there
and she felt it.

She looked over in my direction
but she didn't see me.

Then she drove six cows
back over the hill
and her dress was blowing
this way and that.

I hope that she reads this someday.
I hope that she knows.
I hope that she doesn't show this
to her husband.

OR A THING FOR TAKING STONES OUT OF A DONKEY'S HOOF

I want a holiday from being me.
I want to be a teapot or a paperclip
for a while.
I want to be a clear mountain stream.
I want to be anything
which does not involve
reacting or responding like me.
A snail or an ant or an armadillo.
I want to be a woman called Felicity
or a Tibetan monk.
A fortnight or so as a left shoe
or a left anything at all
would do me a world of good.
From this moment on
until I tell you otherwise
please do not call me Pat.
Kindly put a teabag into me instead
and warm me up first.
I am a teapot until further notice.
A teapot called Sybil Mendoza.
That should do it.

BEHIND YOU

A camera operator
called Rudolph Thwisk
is peering through
his viewfinder
at a couple
watching a picture
on their television
of an old man
watching a video
of a couple
sitting in
a cinema watching
a film of two teenagers
sitting in
their car
watching a huge
drive-in movie screen
on which they can see
a camera operator
called Rudolph Thwisk
peering through
his viewfinder.

THIS POEM IS NOT A HAIKU OR A SONNET OR ANYTHING LIKE THAT BUT PIGEONS LOVE IT

Why do city pigeons never land
on parked cars or motorbikes?
I think it's because
we have got the decency
not to perch up on their ledges.

The worst case ever in the Whole World

Old men love to stop in the street
and tell you all about their
operations.
They love to stop in the street
and light up a cigarette
and explode into a spasm of coughing
which makes the outer rims of their ears
turn purple.
They love to tell you about medical students
who hitched all the way from Siam and India
just to stand around the bed and say –
"My word – this is exceedingly very strange.
  Do you mind if we put your wee wee into bottles
  and preserve it for generations yet to come?"
They love to tell you about surgeons
who opened them up and immediately
called all their friends by mobile phone
and said – "Drop those golf clubs and get round
here fast. This man actually died two years ago
but nobody has told him yet."
The next logical progression
is for old men to operate upon themselves.

Do not encourage them.

BE CAREFUL – YOU MIGHT SAY SOMETHING GOOD
(An actual conversation I had in a shop)

"I like your shirt ... it's brilliant."

"My girlfriend bought it for me."

"She's got very good taste."

"Aw ... she ... she's not bad."

IT'S HARD

I don't think that worms
like concrete very much.

You'd say to yourself
"I think I'll just wriggle
 up top for a while
 and see what's going on."

But you'd come up under
a main road or a runway
and bash your little head
and say – "My goodness
that ground is very hard!"

I don't think that worms
like concrete very much
and I don't blame them.
I only like it myself
when it is fresh and wet
and I can write my name
in it with a stick
when nobody is looking.
Worms never do this
so it's a dead loss
as far as they are
concerned.

The only good thing
about it is
that a hungry blackbird
can't peck his way thro'
and hoist you out by
your tail.

If worms look at it this way
perhaps they won't mind so much.
Blackbirds will though.

BAD TO BETTER

"I hate this bloody birthmark
  on my face."

"My father's one was bigger
  than that."

"Hey – hold on a minute ...
  my one goes all the way round
  the back as well."

MOTHER HALF

If your mother had her way
you would still be playing
with your dolls.
She is denying you your years.
You need to go to all the places
where she isn't.

You need to stick
a vacuum cleaner nozzle
into your ear
and suck her voice
out of your head.

You need to get a mirror
which reflects you
and you only.

Two into you
will not go.
Split yourself
down the middle
and step away
from the other half
      mother half
      will topple
      mother half
      will fall
      down will
      come toxic
      and poison
      and all.

HIGH

After years of being solitary
my life is suddenly filling up
with lots of exciting
and nourishing people
and I am so high
that I cannot sleep or eat
or concentrate or anything.
My mind is whizzing
that way and this.
My head is going much faster
than my legs can.
I can't keep up with me.
I think that very soon
I am going to burst
and I can tell you
it's a much better way to go
than the way I was thinking about
last week.
It will be a glorious heady explosion
with life written all over it.
What a lovely lively way to go.

KILLINEY BEACH 1994

I saw wave after wave
surging in
towards Killiney Beach
and when each one broke
on the shore
part of it
rushed forward
and part of it
sucked at the sand
and churned up shells
and gravel
and made a gurgling sound.
It was beautiful to see.
It was beautiful to hear.

FLASH

I was sitting in Bewleys
in Westmoreland Street
concentrating so hard
on looking cool
that I flicked the ash
off my cigarette
into my cup of coffee.
That's what you get.

EARLY LESSONS IN SELF-ESTEEM

When I was little
and didn't know
too much
about good or bad
there was a prayer
in my prayer book
which taught me
to say –
"I humbly prostrate
    my unworthy
        wretched
            sinful
                self
      in your perfect
          sight."

That was the way to have us.

I'M ONLY THE PERSON YOU'RE ASKING

"Are you enjoying your retirement
  Mister Gavigan?"

"Yes he is"

"Are you making any plans
  now that you've got
  all that free time
  Mister Gavigan?"

"Yes he is"

"Are you suiting yourself now
  Mister Gavigan?"

"Yes he is"

"Do you ever get a word in edgeways
  Mister Gavigan?"

"Of course he does – don't you
  dear?"

"Eh ... yes"

"There ... you see"

LET THIS BE AN END TO IT

You can win The National Lottery
and fall out of a plane
the same day
and land in a combine harvester
which shreds you up
into little sections
and compacts you
into a bale of hay
and all that money
is no good to you.

Why?

Because you haven't got
your health.

And what is your health?

(All together)
"Your health is your wealth."

As well as you are

They let you out of your bed.
You are well enough for that.
The window in your room
only opens so far.

They let you out of your room.
You are well enough for that .
Well enough to wander
past the line of beds
past the women sleeping
deep under covers
past the women awake
and staring straight up
well enough to wander
but only as far
as the locked door
as well as you are
only as far
as the locked door.

Thin and bone
I see you
thin and bone
I feel you
thin and bone
you clench your fists
when you speak
about your mother.

God – you've got so thin.

I see you
beautiful young woman
worn and trembling
moving much too quickly
this way
that way
that way
this way
I embraced you
I felt you
bone and trembling
as well as you are.

I love you.

You asked me
to follow you
and I did
past the beds
past the women
you wanted to show
me something
outside
through the window
a single bird's feather
trapped
on a piece of wire.

"The nurses won't let me
  go out to free it
  they won't let me
  they won't."

You shook
and looked out
at the feather.

I said to you
"When the right wind comes
  the feather will know
  and it will fly."

"And leave me behind?"

"When the right wind comes
  you will know
  and you will fly too."

I don't know
if you believed me.
I said it a second time
because I wanted
to believe myself.

Then I went home
and left you
as well as you are.
Well enough to wander
past the beds
and down as far
as the locked door.

A FRAGILE SORT OF JOY

I am floating
on a most exquisite
island of joy
and if I fall off it
I will drown
in my own tears.

You talk all the time
and you don't listen
and no matter
what anybody says
you know everything
there is to know
about it
and I cannot stand you
because you remind me
so much of myself.

PECK PECK PECK

Sitting in the sun
in North Earl Street
selling my poetry books.
Three street children
standing beside me.

The littlest one
"Give us a smoke Pat"

Fag packet and lighter
on the ground beside me.

"Help yourself"

The littlest guy
takes a cigarette
out of the packet
and lights it.
It is nearly as big
as himself.

The next biggest guy
whips it out of
his mouth.

"I'll give you the butt"

He scarcely has time
to take a puff.

The biggest guy
whips it out
of his mouth.

"I'll give you the butt"

Off they go
up the street.
The biggest guy
smoking.
The littlest guy
  and the next
    littlest guy
walking alongside him
waiting for a puff
        or a drag
        or a butt
or whatever else
it pleased him
to give them.

I thought it was
a hitchhiker
walking past
until I took
a closer look
and realised
that it was
a huge big
rucksack
with legs.
They were suntanned
and everything.

"Excuse me" I said.
"Forgive me for asking
  but you're not really
  a hitchhiker are you?"

"How very observant
  of you to notice"
said the rucksack
and it danced
a little jig for joy
and rattled
its saucepans.
And I danced too.
Yahoo!

A Stranger in Your Shoes

If you smile
though your
heart
is breaking
there is
no point
looking into
a mirror.

You will
only see
someone else.

PLEASE DON'T BE MUCH LONGER

Loneliness is hurting me
with a bad pain today.
It is a sick feeling
in my stomach.
It is a lot of tears
pressing behind my eyes.

Someday the right person
will come
and hold me.
Someday the right person
will come
and say
"I know how you are
  I know who you are
  I am here now
  I care."

Someday the right person
will come
and give something to me.
I am very tired of waiting.
I am very tired of wanting.
I am very tired.
Please come soon.

I WOULDN'T BELIEVE ANYBODY IF THEY TOLD ME THIS
BUT EVERY WORD IS TRUE – HONESTLY IT IS ... I SWEAR

I started to wonder.
My bus was nearing
the railway bridge
at Clontarf.

"I wonder how many times
  I'll have to go under
  this bridge before
  I see a train going
  over it."
And God Almighty
even as I thought it
I saw one.
I saw a train.
I was thrilled.

As the bus neared
the next bridge
at Fairview
I started to think
"I wonder what are
  the chances of
  seeing another one."
And may I drop dead
if I tell a lie
I saw another train.
I am not making this up.
I swear it.

My heart raced.
My blood pumped.
Two trains in a row.
Holy shit.

As my bus was nearing
the railway bridge
over the North Strand
I was holding my breath.
No ... no ... it's not possible.
Three trains in a row ...
no chance ...
a million to one ...
quit while you're ahead ...
Then
all of a glorious sudden
A TRAIN!!
YES! YES! YES!
I was ecstatic.
I was trembling.
THIS INDEED IS WHY
I WAS BORN!

My bus was nearing
the railway bridge
over Talbot Street.
I was out of control.
Out of my head
with trains.

This time
I didn't think
anything.
I just looked.
I just looked.
And glory of glories!
The impossible dream!
The multiple miracle!
Another magnificent
clickedy clacking
rolling rolling
train!

The last time
I felt like this
they gave me lithium.
The last time
I felt like this
I levitated
amongst the seagulls
over Howth Head.
Four bridges.
Four trains.
What a glorious
sight to see.
Four bridges.
Four trains.
What a glorious time
to be me.

MORE OF ME

I eat Jaffa Cakes in bed
at four o'clock in the morning
when I am lonely.

I eat lots of them
and they make my stomach fat.

I like to think
that I am growing
some more of me
to keep myself company.

A Parable from the Streets

told to me by Bren

"I was walkin' down the street
and I hadn't got a butt
or the price of a drink
or anything
and I seen this purse
and I picked it up
and I said
'The blessings of Jaysus
 on whoever lost it'
there was £342 in it
so I went to the off-licence
and I bought a flagon
and a bottle of gin
and I supped off some of the cider
and I mixed in some of the gin
and I sat down against a wall
and I was drinking it
and I swear to God
the people started lashing
money at me
loads of pound coins
and everything.
I'm telling you
when you have fuck all
        you get fuck all."

STUMPED

If self-praise is no praise
I cannot imagine what is.

IRISH COMPLIMENT

"I saw your little television programme
... by accident ...
and I have to give you this much ...
you're not the worst of them."

That is as good as it's going to get.

MONIKA

A radiant smile
of dizzy joy
eyes sparkling
bright and giddy
with excitement
is how I see you
seeing me
this morning.
I am drunk
with the delight
of it.

WIPE OUT

My front door slammed
so hard in the wind
that all the letters
in all the books
on my shelves
fell out
and cascaded
onto the floor.
I opened my bottle
of Tippex
and waved
the little
white brush
in the air.

"If you're not
  back inside
  those books
  when I count
  up to ten
  I'll correct
  the lot of you!"

WHOOOOSH!

WORDS OF LOVE

The Dublin mammy
looked lovingly
into the pram
and said –
"How's Mammy's
  scruffy little
  bastard!?"
And the baby gurgled
with delight.

It's all in the way
that you say it.

IRELAND ABU!

Let us sing
and dance
and praise them
now that they're
decently dead.
Joyce, Wilde,
Kavanagh
let us quote
the things
they said.
Seminars
Summer Schools
Lectures,
Academics
making hay
cash registers
ting-a-ling
DEAD WRITERS
RULE O.K.!

VERY VERY VERY VERY VERY VERY FEW PEOPLE WILL EVER TELL YOU THIS

You don't need permission to be free.

Some little girls hold
their mother's hand
and adventure around
the town.
Some little girls hold
a tray of lighters
and shout
"Five for a pound."

MY FAVOURITE FIVE WORDS ... TWICE

DURING THE DAY   "How much is your book?"

AFTER DARK   "Can I stay the night?"

LITTLE LIGHTER GIRL KNOWS

A little Dublin girl
aged about 8 or 9
who was selling
lighters
stopped and looked
at my poetry books
spread out on the ground.

"Hey mister - are
  you selling them?"

"Yes I am."

"How much are they?"

"A fiver each."

She glanced over
all the books
very quickly
once.

"If you sell all them
  you'll get £165."

It took me over one
minute to check.

She was absolutely right.

BILLY THE KID AND JESSE JAMES

Last night after dark
I, the keeper of an unlicensed television set
was almost knocked down and killed
by a helmetless cyclist
who was riding an unlit bike on the footpath.
What a daring pair of lawbreakers are we!

Keep this to Yourself

The woman with
staring eyes
on the bus
told me that
she writes
all Bruce
Springsteen's
songs.

"I write them
  in the key of C
  and I put them
  in the shoebox
  under my bed."

"How does Bruce
  Springsteen
  get them?"

"I think it's
  the son of the
  woman I live
  with. He has
  a long ladder."

My God – supposing
this is true ...

WELL GONE

"What time is the next bus please?"

"19.32."

"Jesus – I'll never get that...
  it's ten years before I was born."

IT ALL COMES DOWN TO PROFIT

I don't feel comfortable
in the same room
as business men.
They make me uneasy.
They love dividing things
in two and giving you
the little bit.
They love percentages
preferably 60, 70, 80, 90
or 100 if they can get it.

Only one percentage deal
really interests me.
If I am hungry
I would like you to give me
half of your dinner.
If you are hungry
I will do the same.

You don't need a calculator for that.

LITTLE MISS SINGLE SNOWFLAKE

I love the single snowflake
which twirls down into white silence
moments after the main snowfall
has stopped.
If I was a woman
that is how I would arrive
at the ball.

View from a train in November

The trees are twig-thin
bare black
cold as shaky bones.
They hide nothing now.
Blades of grass are stiff
in the fields.
Earth and clay
are concrete hard
and grip frozen water
between rough ridges.
A man's breath is cold cloud.
He walks down one side
of an empty ditch
and up the other.
Half a moon is high
although it is not yet night.
The tips of things
are frozen with the frost.

Three young uniformed gardai
raced down North Earl Street
and burst into Anne's Coffee
Shop.
The guy they were chasing
wasn't in there.
20 minutes later
I went in for a coffee
and mentioned the drama
to the woman behind
the counter.
"You must have been freaked"
I said.
She shook her head.
"It's my birthday today"
she said.
"I thought it was a Kissogram."

PAMPER ME BOTTOM

Little chubby baby
grabbing at your toes
bouncy little bundle
chookey button nose
do not distress yourself
please do not cry
technology is working
tirelessly
to keep your bottom dry.

There is No Excuse for an Anti-Climax Like This

The stranger walked into the farmyard.
He seemed to be searching for something.
He looked at the cows and shook his head.
He noticed a couple of ducks.
"No ... no ... not them."
"I bet it's me" said the horse.
"Not you either" the stranger said.
He dismissed the pigs
    rejected the goats
    ignored the donkey.
He was just about to leave the farmyard
dejected
morose
melancholy
suicidal
when at last HE SAW ONE.
His spirits soared.
His heart rejoiced.
He exulted inwardly.
He rushed over to the goose and he said it.
"Boo!"

IT ISN'T

She said
"I was waiting
  at a bus stop
  when a rhinoceros
  came rampaging
  along the Clontarf Road
  and I wasn't wearing
  my glasses
  so I thrust out my hand
  to stop it
  but it thundered on past.
"Did you see that?"
I said to the very
short squat man
beside me.
"The bus didn't stop.'
"You'll have to excuse me"
he said. "I'm not wearing
my glasses. But as far
as I could see
you were attempting
to hail a haystack
with legs."
Then she put on
her glasses
and discovered that
she had been conversing
with a litter bin.
He put on his glasses
and discovered that
she wasn't there
at all.

OVER THE EDGE

Although it might look like it
from the far distance
the horizon is not in fact
the edge of the world.
It is actually a sheer drop
of 200,000 feet
into Mrs. Moriarty's back garden.
She is not very happy about this
because huge big ships
frequently fall down
onto her patio
with an unmerciful crash
while she is playing chess
with Rupert Netherby.
"Fuck it anyway Rupert"
she exclaims.
"There's another ship."
"You really should complain
  to somebody" says Rupert.
"I would if I thought they
  were doing it on purpose."
she replies.
Night time is the worst.
All the sailors shout
"Avast belay"
and hoot their sirens
and fire bright rockets.
I don't know how she
puts up with it.
Perhaps she is glad
of the company.

OH GOD

I spied out
at the car ferry
through
the wrong end
of my binoculars
and it became
so tiny
that a seagull
dropped a shell
and sank it.

SOMEBODY'S DAUGHTER

She has learned
how to place
a plastic bag
on the ground
and sit on it
and rest her
back against
a litter bin
and place
her anorak
flat in front
of her
and put a piece
of cardboard
on her lap
with the words
"Hungry
  Homeless
  Please help"
on it
and blow a
cheap tin whistle
over and over
again
and she
is only seven.

A Single to Me

What it is to wander
and look at towns
and sit on trains
and wish there was
someone you could
talk with.

What it is to wander
and sleep alone
and eat alone
and wish there was
someone you could
laugh with.

What it is to sit
on a little empty
station waiting for
the first train
to somewhere
and wish there was
someone to whom
you could say
"Isn't the birdsong
  beautiful."

What it is to go
as far north in Scotland
as the train will take you
and discover that it isn't
nearly far enough.

What it is to be here
and not want to go home
and be home and not want
to be here.

It is time for me to buy
a ticket to myself.

The worn-out bent-down
weary walking woman
picked and pecked
and poked around
the empty tables
picked and pecked
like a ravenous gull
tested cardboard cups
poked among the plates
rummaged under
crumpled tissues
found a crust
and wolfed it
found a dregs
and drank it.
All around her
heat and light
and music piped
heat and light
and plenty
heat and light
and music piped
ragged stomach
empty.

GOTCHA

At first he wasn't sure.
He couldn't swear to it.
The woman's navel appeared
to be speaking to him.
Not out loud.
It was shaping words very clearly
like a television newsreader for the Deaf.
"Hello" it said. "I'm a navel."
He had to be extra-specially careful.
He didn't want the woman to see him
addressing her bare midriff.
He chose the right moment and
carefully mimed his reply.
"Hi - I'm Geoffrey."
"Do ... do you think I'm a nice navel?"
"Stop - this is much too dangerous."
"I love you Geoffrey."
"Fuck off."
The navel puckered its lips and made
a passionate kissing sound.
"Stop that" said the woman
without even looking down.
"Stop that at once
  or I'll bung in your cork."
A little tear rolled out of the navel
and trickled down the woman's tummy.
Another one followed.
Then another.

"Madam" said the man. I feel
  personally responsible for your
  wet stomach."
"Well lick it dry then" she said.
"Lick it dry."
Which indeed he did.
And more.
Much much more.
Once again
effortlessly
with practised ease
Madam Nina Vespucci
and her incredible crying stomach
had snared another victim.

I'M NOT SURE ABOUT ICEBERGS THOUGH

I love people
who cycle after dark
with red winkey lights
on their backs.
Ships will never
bump into them.

HONESTLY

Under the late light of a pale moon
when there was nobody around to see
a very tall construction-site crane
leaned over the top of Virgin Records
bent its long neck down
and took a drink out of the Liffey.
Please don't tell anyone.
You'll only get it into trouble.

A little hidden bird
sang to me a secret
in the twilight hour
after sunset.

"Pssst Pat ...
promise you won't
tell anyone ......"

"I promise."

"O.K. Listen very
carefully. I'll
only sing this once.
Humpty Dumpty faked it.
It was really a lookalike
egg from South America -
Ricardo 'Two-Yolks'
Suarez Sanchez."

Do you ever know?

CRUSTY

Crusty rolls give out hell
to all the other bread
in the bakery.
Crusty rolls intimidate
the batch loaves
and bully
the curranty buns.
Crusty rolls are afraid
of being remaindered
as 'Yesterday's Bread.'
That is what they secretly dread.
Please don't ignore them.
Fair enough
they might be grumpy
little fuckers
but please don't buy
a Vienna Roll instead.
You'll only make them worse.
You'll only make them mutter
and curse and insult
the curranty buns
when no-one is looking.
Crusty rolls are afraid
of going soft.
It might be the best thing for them.

AMANDA WAS A TOURIST GUIDE

She didn't last long
as a tourist guide
which is a pity
because her commentaries
were rich and vivid and varied.
She didn't last long
as a tourist guide
because everytime
she pointed her finger
at a famous old building
it fell down.
Sometimes
it didn't collapse entirely.
The roof caved in
or huge lumps of masonry
crashed down from the top.
That was nearly as bad.
She demolished
pre-Christian sites
Georgian houses
Norman castles.
She simply pointed her finger
and they fell down.
She didn't last long
as a tourist guide
which is a pity
because her commentaries
were rich and vivid and varied.
She works in an office now.
Nothing ever falls down.
There is nothing
she wants to point at.

HANG IN THERE

The bus driver took off
from the stop
so suddenly
that he left
the upper deck behind.
It hovered in mid-air
and people looked out
through the windows
not realising
that there was
no lower deck
beneath them.
If you are reading this
on the upper deck of a bus
open one of the windows
ask a fellow passenger
to hold onto your feet
and dangle you down outside.
If you can see the lower deck
there is absolutely nothing
to worry about.
If you can't see it
you are travelling on the bus
in this poem.
I'm off to bed now
so good luck.

The achiever's lament

I can
specify quantify
classify verify
modify
but I don't know how
to talk to my children.

I can
motivate dictate
update delegate
activate
but I don't know how
to talk to my children.

I can rationalise decimalise
analyse capitalise
marginalise
but I don't know how
to talk to my children.

SERVES HIM RIGHT

I knew this fellah
and he smoked 80 a day
and he ate tons
of greasy foods
and he never took
any exercise
and he wore
damp clothes
and he sat
in draughts
and do you know
something?
He died when
he was 18.

When the big black things
started to scream at her
Gretchen Cranny stayed
in the house.
When the big black things
started to look in
through her windows
Gretchen Cranny pulled
the curtains.
When the little lonely things
started to move around
inside her stomach
Gretchen Cranny talked
to the people
on her television.
She told the man
who reads the news
all about the big black things
screaming outside her house.
She told the woman
on the weather forecast
all about the little lonely things
inside her stomach.
The woman on the weather forecast
told her to get a bread knife
and let them out.

Three days have passed.

Tomorrow a garda will find
Gretchen Cranny.

He will turn off the television.
He will put the bread knife
into a plastic bag.
He will not find
the little lonely things.
They are all gone now.
Gretchen Cranny let them out.

When you wish to write a poem now
you have to sit at a clacky keyboard
and it's all computerised.
Nobody remembers
what a pen was anymore.
"A what? ... Oh ... a pen ...
  they had one of those
  in the travelling
  exhibition.
  They had a book too...
  with pages and a cover
  and everything.
  At least I think
  that's what it was. "

When you wish to paint a picture now
you have to sit at a clacky keyboard
and it's all computerised.
Nobody remembers
what a brush was anymore.
The man over at Keyboard Unit 7
saw one once.
At least he thinks it was a brush.
It might have been a pen though.
It had bristles.
What was that?
A pen or a brush?
It might have been a pencil.
They had bristles...
I think.

If you wish to protest now
you have to sit at a clacky keyboard
and enter your protest.
You could write it up on a wall
if you had a pen or a brush
or a tin of paint.
You could write it up on a wall
if you knew how to write or paint.

I have just finished
writing these words on
my portable manual typewriter.

I hear footsteps outside my door.

How do people Know?

There is a crucial point
during take-off
at which the pilot
cannot pull back
even if he wants to.
There is a similar point
when I am sitting
on the toilet
doing a hefty.
It is at this
precise moment
that my phone rings.
I hate that.

SHARP CUT

Silver fish peeped out of the water.
It was sharp green.
It was sharp green enough
to slice a lemon.
Silver fish peeped out of the water
and fired hot beams of light
up out of their eyes.
The beams criss-crossed
and cut black squares
out of the sky.
Golden light flamed.
Liquid fire fell.
The sea hissed and steamed
and melted the eyes
of the silver fish.
They sank blind
into the sharp green.
Green enough to slice a lemon.

A THANK YOU TO MY SKIN

Thank you, go raibh maith agat, merci, skin.
for keeping all my squelchy bits in.

PICTURES IN THE ROAD

The rain flooded down
and placed a deep black mirror
in the road.
A man walking past
on the far pavement
didn't know that his head
and his head alone
was moving upside down
across the edges
of the pool.
The traffic lights
threw red and green and orange
in amongst the upside down
chimneys.
A car stopped and stood directly
over a perfect picture of itself.
A cyclist cut through
the middle of the mirror
and wiped the pictures away
with sideways surges of water.
When the surges settled
the world was upside down again.
The traffic lights
threw red and green and orange
in amongst the chimneys.

Twixt in Twain

The screaming whine of the engine
under the back seat of the bus
became a silver sharp wheel
which spun upwards
and cut the man
into two perfect halves.
One half of the man
held my notebook
and the other half of him
wrote these words down for me.

THE RIM OF HIM

The very edges of him
the very rim of him
detached itself
from his body
and crept away
while he wasn't looking.

The very edges of him
the very rim of him
rolled around
in chalk dust
until it looked like
a white line drawing
of the man.

Late that night
it crept back
while he was sleeping
and spreadeagled itself
on the pavement
outside his house.

Next morning
when he saw
the white outline
marked against the ground
he said — "My goodness —
somebody must have been
shot here last night."

He lay down flat
to check the white shape
and said — "Good heavens —
that somebody was me ...
I wonder what they did
with the body."

The white outline
sprang up suddenly
and raced away
leaving him
lying there
without any edges ...
wondering ....

THESE PICTURES WANT ME TO PAINT THEM

Words are not enough today.
Wild pictures are screaming
against the insides of my head
and trying to burst out
through my fingertips.

A tall thin man
with no face
is standing up
very straight
in a wide white field.
A red express train
is coming out through
a hole in his chest.

Black birdsong is chattering
through a wire fence
and vibrating the bone
of my head.
Black birdsong is chattering
"Mix me in with
  dogs barking
  drills whining
  hammers thudding
  and make new music
  with me."

White marble blades
are standing up straight
in a white marble field.

Bulging balloons
are dropping down
and exploding open
and flinging
bright red flashes
this way and that way
and everyway.
The white marble is dripping
with crimson.

To change these words
into real pictures
and mix them in
with sharp music
would be a wonderful
and a terrifying thing.

Peace is on the other side.

It's O.K.

Be calm, be quiet, be still.
You are here now.
Listen to your breathing.
Be safe, be sure, be here.
Tomorrow can never touch you.
Feel the ground with your feet.
This is where you are.
There is nothing else
for you to deal with.
Look ... here.
What do you see?
Listen ... here.
What do you hear?
Touch ... here.
What do you feel?
There is nothing else.
It is not possible
            to see
            or hear
            or feel
      anywhere else.
Be here.
Be safe.
Be now.
Be you.

SANCTUARY

Did you know that
delinquent ducks
and cheeky geese
sneak out of the bird sanctuary
in Booterstown
and creep across
the road
and rat tat tat
on people's
front doors
and windows
and then
leg it back
into the
sanctuary
and stick
their fingers
on their noses
and make faces
at the people
and say "Bah
Jeery Bah
You Can't
Touch Us!"

Cheeky little fuckers.

WITHOUT MY CLACK

The train was passing
over the railway bridge
in Pearse Street
with a lovely rhythmic
clickedy clack
clickedy clack
clickedy clack
and me standing
under the bridge
grooving inside my head
with a lovely rhythmic
clickedy clack
clickedy clack
clickedy clack
when all of a sudden
the last carriages
passed over the bridge
with an unforgiveable
clickedy clack
clickedy clack
clickedy......
There was no final clack.
What a terrible thing
for a train to do
to anybody
leaving me standing there
feeling incomplete
leaving me standing there
with a clack missing.

I waited for ages
hoping for a train
which had a clack to spare.
I waited for ages
hoping for a train
with an extra clack
to make me whole again.

A missing clack
or a missing anything
at all
can follow you
long after the last train
has gone.

Didn't it get dark
didn't it.
Didn't everybody go away
didn't they.
Didn't it get so quiet
and empty
that you could
fall into it
forever
didn't it.
Didn't you say nothing
to anyone
for so long
that you wondered
if you would ever
be able to make words
again
didn't you.
And the phone didn't ring.
And the phone didn't ring.
And the phone didn't ring.
And it will get light again
won't it.
And I will see people again
won't I.
And I will meet you
for the very first time
won't I.

LET ME WITH GENTLENESS

Let me kiss your breasts
till both of us
are dizzy.
Let me lick your secret
place
till you are groaning
with the agony
of too much pleasure
and my tongue is drowning
in your juices.

HOLD ON HOLD OFF

How do people
find other people
to walk hand
in hand with?
There are loads
of people
doing it.
They're everywhere.
They're holding hands.
They're holding fingers.
Sometimes
they're holding other
bits as well.
I wish that once a week
there was a 'National
No-Holding-Anything-At-
All-Day'.
I wouldn't feel so bad then.